A SELECTION of POEMS

A SELECTION
of
POEMS

Jane McIntosh Holland

A selection of poems

Copyright © 2019 by Jane Mcintosh Holland. All rights reserved.

No part of this publication may be reproduced, stored in a retrieval system or transmitted in any way by any means, electronic, mechanical, photocopy, recording or otherwise without the prior permission of the author except as provided by USA copyright law.

This novel is a work of fiction. Names, descriptions, entities, and incidents included in the story are products of the author's imagination. Any resemblance to actual persons, events, and entities is entirely coincidental.

The opinions expressed by the author are not necessarily those of URLink Print and Media.

1603 Capitol Ave., Suite 310 Cheyenne, Wyoming USA 82001
1-888-980-6523 | admin@urlinkpublishing.com

URLink Print and Media is committed to excellence in the publishing industry.

Book design copyright © 2019 by URLink Print and Media. All rights reserved.

Published in the United States of America
ISBN 978-1-64367-508-4 (Paperback)
ISBN 978-1-64367-507-7 (Digital)

15.05.19

I would like to dedicate the book and all of my
books to my parents and my ex husband
who are no longer alive.

George McIntosh Holland, my dad Margret
Ruth Holland, my mum

Peter Douglas, my ex husband

Contents

Sea Shells 2

The Sunflower 4

The Two Mischievous Cats 6

Lizzie My Beautiful Cat 8

Out Of Tune 9

Time In Which We Share 10

The Endless Road 11

The White Rose 13

Manly 15

The Kangaroo 17

The Kelpie 19

Pickles The Cat 21

The Flower 22

SEA SHELLS

Sea Shells upon the beach on the sand. We walk on them and listen to them with our ears, and smell them with our nose.
They are all different and, are the home of much sea life.
The sea shells come in different shapes and sizes, and live under the sea and brought to shore along by the tide along the coast.

THE SUNFLOWER

The sunflower stands straight to the sun; it appears straight and tall, following the sun in all its glory.
The Bee buzzes around collecting pollen for the hive; this helps more flowers grow.
The sunflower grows up to the sky along with the others in the garden, the rain waters the ground and helps them grow.
Plentiful is the flower bed, the smell is overpowering and floats upon the air.

THE TWO MISCHIEVOUS CATS

Pickles and Lizzie two mischievous cats play in the sunlight chasing
their tails the shadows and a leaf.
Playing chasing up the hallway, very frisky, enjoying their life.
Pickles and Lizzie mischievous cats chase the mice and they are
barked at by dogs.
Living among the gum trees and the wattle.

LIZZIE MY BEAUTIFUL CAT

My cat Lizzie was a very special girl the day I brought her home she began to purr.
Each day was an adventure with this mischievous madam she was silver in colour very intelligent and a fantastic hunter and a wonderful companion.
Lizzie the cat lived with me amongst the gum trees and the bottle brush trees.
Lizzie was a rescue cat from the city she had already been desexed so I didn't have to worry about the patter of other kittens.
She lived with me for three years at my old residents she helped me through my suffering with arthritis and made everything more bearable.
Then we moved up the road to Manly still amongst the gum trees.
Lizzie and I settled in quite well she loved her new home and our new neighbors and Casper the white tom cat.
Eventually I acquired another kitten and she was a tortishell and very beautiful just like Lizzie. It took a while for Lizzie to accept Pickles but with hard work they got better.
I miss Lizzie very much for she went missing before I went into hospital. I put signs around asked my friends but she was gone I still have Pickles and I love her so but I miss my silver lady very much my good friend.

OUT OF TUNE

I sit in the sunroom year after year
Dust accumulating in every crack.
My wood creaks
My keys are broken, and out of tune.
The family photos on my top
Are faded by the sun.
I am polished occasionally by mum.
But in the corner I remain with
The sounds of the family surrounding me.
I have been played by the girls and by dad
But as the grew up and moved out
They lost interest in me.
Father bought an electric organ and he plays it now
Progress I suspect
But if only they would tune me, then maybe they would play me.
So until then here I remain an unplayed upright, spending his days in the sun.
PS: I suppose it could be worse, at least I'm not the poor violin in the closet.

TIME IN WHICH WE SHARE

Time in which we share
Living together is the joy we bring.
Pain occaisonally surrounds us
It cannot pass us by.
New relatives and relations
Will join in the fair.
We scream and shout and laugh about
Without a care.
Our lives we share
The joy we care and all the
Laughter within.

THE ENDLESS ROAD

The endless road winds its way through living together
Is the joy we new.
Day after day lives and loves, people come and go
Animals come and go.
Trees come and go
The air is salty the sky is blue
The clouds are white
And all is new.
You drive a car
Along the endless road
To nowhere but you
But you end up somewhere.
The coast road is endless
The sky is endless life is endless
Life goes on
You lose friends and family
Along the way
But you'll meet them again someday.
Time is sweet the sun is warm
The water is cool
The salt on your skin.
Your cat licks the salt off Your body
days begin days end
And the endless road
Winds its way through
To the end.

THE WHITE ROSE

The white rose sits in a vase
Beautiful and clean.
The white rose smells fresh
Silent and pure
On its stem are thorns
You must take care.
The white rose is amazing
To behold, made by nature watered by the rain
And a seed in the garden
Planted by love and care
The White rose is love and peace.

Manly Corso Summer Time Our Christmas

MANLY

Beach town friendly people, the corso
And Manly ferry takes you to the city.
Everyone comes to Manly home of the sea eagles
Footy team.
Meat pies and fish and chips don't feed the seagulls
They will attack you.
Manly is my home town on the Northern beaches
Of Sydney Town.
The name Manly came because the aborigines were bigger in size.
Manly sunny and carefree lifestyle.
Manly is the best unlike the rest
My home town I could not live anywhere else.
I will love Manly all of my days.

THE KANGAROO

The kangaroo jumps and jumps over the bush in the heat and the dust
The kangaroo bounds across the wide land with other kangaroos along the way.
The kangaroo enjoys his life along the bush track amongst the gum trees the wattle and the bottle brush trees.
Sounds of the other animals in the bush.
The kangaroo flys across the wide land happy and carefree in the rain and the sun they have much fun.
The kangaroo is on the Quanta's plane, represents our country.
The kangaroo is Skippy the bush kangaroo.
The kangaroo is a beautiful animal carries its baby in its pouch.
The kangaroo is brown or red little or big, there is the tree kangaroo or the wallaby they get killed or injured on the road by the big trucks that drive throughout this country.
They get resuced by dedicated people who help to get them better and back to the bush.
The kangaroo is Australia and Australia is the kangaroo throughout the land they are part of us our home.

THE KELPIE

Sheep dog works hard with its master lives to work and to please its master
The kelpie loyal and smart Australian working dog loves to chase balls
and frisbees very fit and lean you can have a cross kelpie or a red
kelpie but whatever the colour they are great dogs
I had one myself his name was spot and he loved me and my dad. He
lived a good long life and died at my father's house I still have photos
of spot and my dad I miss them both.

PICKLES THE CAT

Tortishell female my friend my companion she lives with me in my flat in Manly she loves her food
And to chase a cat ball around the flat she is my main pet now as I lost another cat recently and now I just have Pickles she is a pretty girl and I love her so.
Pickles the tortishell cat what a great life she has.

THE FLOWER

In the garden
The bees hover above green leaves surround the flowers
Leaves on the ground birds in the sky the flowers make the garden colourful all sorts of
Flowers in the garden daisy, rose, blossom plant a bulb and water the plant and eventually you get a flower for people to see and make the air smell sweet.
The flower blooms in the sunlight near a pond or a creek makes the earth beautiful.